IMAGES OF NATURE

Canadian Poets and the Group of Seven

J. E. H. MacDonald, *Leaves in the Brook*

Compiled by David Booth

Kids Can Press Ltd.

Toronto

TO MARY MACCHIUSI

Kids Can Press Ltd. acknowledges with appreciation the assistance of the Canada Council and the Ontario Arts Council in the production of this book.

Canadian Cataloguing in Publication Data

Main entry under title:

Images of nature : Canadian poets and the Group of Seven

Includes index.

ISBN 1-55074-272-8

1. Children's poetry, Canadian (English) — 20th century.*
2. Nature — Juvenile poetry. 3. Nature (Aesthetics).
4. Painting, Canadian. 5. Painting, Modern —
20th century — Canada. I. Booth, David.

PS8293.I53   1995   jC811'.5408'036   C95-930615-3
PZ8.3.I53   1995

Kids Can Press Ltd.
29 Birch Avenue
Toronto, Ontario, Canada
M4V 1E2

Edited by Charis Wahl
Designed by Marie Bartholomew
Printed and bound in Hong Kong

95 0 9 8 7 6 5 4 3 2 1

A.Y. Jackson, *The Edge of the Maple Wood*

INTRODUCTION

A.J. Casson, *White Pine*

Throughout my life I have been aware of paintings by the Group of Seven — on bank walls, in school halls and on postage stamps. There was never any doubt about the images of these trees of autumn, the shield of rock, the fields of winter; in them I recognized my country, bigger and bolder than I had known in my small town, but nonetheless a panorama of my Canadian dreams. Later, as I learned more about the artists and their work, these paintings came to represent my personal thoughts and feelings about this nation that sprawls across the top of the map. The Group captured the natural heart of Canada and wrapped me in its vision as if inside the flag.

The Canadian poems in this book echo the paintings; the words filter through the artists' pine trees like a loon's call. Each time I read the poems and look at the pictures, I understand more deeply my country and my identity.

When my son attends camp in Northern Ontario this summer, he will paddle his canoe right into a painting by one of the Group of Seven. The hills and trees and rocks will be reflected in the clear lake waters, and the ripples from his paddle will disturb the scene, altering what he sees. As you view the paintings and read the poems in this book, your images of Canada, too, will constantly change, as these artists and poets interpret the sights and sounds of our country. Not with camera and recorder but with brush and pen, they make us look anew and remember forever the power of this land.

DAVID BOOTH

KEEP QUITE STILL

Puff and drift from those far chimneys
where old fashioned men with shovels
bank their fires

will reach you if you
keep quite still
if you

let tendrils of air
find one nostril and another
and what they bring

offering and gift of memory
form in the blood
to recitations of the ticking clock

coal smoke releasing fragrance
of long ago forests
whose birds spread their songs like wings

listen

keep quite
still

JOHN V. HICKS

TRAVEL THE TRAIL OF FIRE

Travel the trail of fire—
In your soul you should remember.
Seated on the sacred blanket
The smoke of the cedar fire
With the drink of herbs
The chant of travel.

I am going to travel the trail of fire.
I am travelling the fire trail.

Far away I heard an owl
        cry
my name
            I heard
my brother   Listen
        shout to me
so I can find you
        in the forest   so I can find
        you
Listen

ORVILLE KEON

Tom Thomson,
Northern River

NOTES ON A NORTHERN LAKE

Rainy River Country,
Northwestern Ontario

1.
We freeze in our beds
The wind sends shivers across the lake

2.
We swelter in the open air
The sun sends lava across the lake

3.
We move among the trees
And through the woods the lake moves too

JOHN ROBERT COLOMBO

Lawren S. Harris, *Montreal River*

NORTH STREAM

Ice mothers me
My bed is rock
Over sand I move silently.

I am crystal clear
To a sunbeam.
No grasses grow in me
My banks are clean.

Foam runs from the rapid
To rest on my dark pools.

F.R. SCOTT

MUNCHAUSEN IN ALBERTA

Our first winter in the settlement,
the old man said,
January was so cold
the flames in the lamp froze.
The women picked them like strawberries
and gave them to the children to eat.

That's the only time
I was ever a fire-eater.

ELIZABETH BREWSTER

WINTER WALK IN FOREST

All else
is so
perfectly still
my breathing sounds
like gusts of wind
my joints
like frozen branches
cracking

All around me
invisible animals
must also be listening

But only
to how close
my boots
snap the snowcrust

GEORGE SWEDE

Lawren S. Harris, *Above Lake Superior*

opposite: Lawren S. Harris, *Snow II*

Tom Thomson, *Wildflowers*

SUMMER HAIKU

For Frank and Marian Scott

Silence
and a deeper silence
when the crickets
hesitate

LEONARD COHEN

SUMMER

Sun bends down
lilacs stirred by wind:
each leaf holds up
the whole sky. A warbler,
brief fruit, shakes loose
a rush of blue.

ROBERT MELANÇON
(TR. PHILIP STRATFORD)

10

J.E.H. MacDonald, *The Tangled Garden*

ELLESMERELAND I

Explorers say that harebells rise
from the cracks of Ellesmereland
and cod swim fat beneath the ice
that grinds its meagre sands
No man is settled on that coast
The harebells are alone
Nor is there talk of making man
from ice cod bell or stone

1952
EARLE BIRNEY

ELLESMERELAND II

And now in Ellesmereland there sits
a town of twenty men
They guard the floes that reach to the Pole
a hundred leagues and ten
These warders watch the sky watch them
the stricken hills eye both
A mountie visits twice a year
and there is talk of growth

1965
EARLE BIRNEY

THE EARTH AND THE PEOPLE

The earth was here before the people.
The very first people
came out of the ground.
Everything came from the ground,
even caribou.
Children once grew
out of the ground
just as flowers do.
Women out wandering
found them sprawling on the grass
and took them home and nursed them.
That way people multiplied.

This land of ours
has become habitable
because we came here
and learned how to hunt.

INUIT TRADITIONAL SONG

F. H. Varley, *Above Arctic Bay*

F. H. Varley, *Eskimo Tents – Cape Dorset*

A.Y. Jackson, *Algoma, November*

FALL

Winter broke over the hill with ice on its breath
Gripped and choked the corn stubble in October.
    ("Early," she said.)
A beaver's shadow stealthily shrank into the rushes
Shivering and lost.
    ("Where is the warm rain
    For soaking and filling the lake?")

Snow! Snow high in the dead fir's fork
Flies wild, swirls on the wind's bite
Grating the teeth and the chilled nerve's end.
    ("Will there be time
    For a walk before dark?")

A last grey goose fluttered its white wings spliced
                    with frost
To fall back squawking in a flurry of sleet.
    ("It's late!")

      It's late on the bitter wind
        In the Fall of this year.

RICHARD COURTNEY

A.Y. Jackson, *Maple Woods, Algoma*

AESTHETIC CURIOSITY

Does an owl appreciate
The colors of leaves
As they fall about him
In the staggering nights of Autumn?

A.M. KLEIN

i dreem uv northern skies i dreem uv northern skies
i dreem uv northern skies i dreem uv northern skies
i dreem uv northern skies i dreem uv northern skies
i dreem uv northern skies i dreem uv northern skies
i dreem uv northern skies i dreem uv northern skies
i dreem uv northern skies i dreem uv northern skies
i dreem uv northern skies i dreem uv northern skies
i dreem uv northern skies i dreem uv northern skies
i dreem uv northern skies i dreem uv northern skies
stars shining evree wher   i dreem uv northern skies
flying buffalo thistul down bed i dreem uv northern skies
skies i dreem uv northern skies i dreem uv northern
skies i dreem uv northern skies i dreem uv northern
skies i dreem uv northern skies i dreem uv northern
skies i dreem uv northern skies i dreem uv northern
skies i dreem uv northern skies i dreem uv northern
skies i dreem th fire rising into the cloud th lake
melting into our heart stars shining evree wher eye
dreem uv northern skies i dreem uv northern skies i
dreem uv northern skies i dreem uv northern skies i
dreem uv northern skies i dreem uv northern skies i
dreem uv northern skies i dreem uv northern skies i
dreem uv northern skies i dreem uv northern skies i
folds i dreem uv northern skies stars shining evree
wher i dreem uv northern sky   foxes deep in th erth
the sereen stars turning ovr th ice dreem uv northern
skies i dreem uv northern skies i dreem uv northern
stars i dreem uv northern skies i dreem uv northern
skies

bill bissett

16

Tom Thomson, *Summer Day*

Franklin Carmichael, *Mirror Lake*

HAIKU

Dropping stone after stone
into the lake   I keep
reappearing

GEORGE SWEDE

Tom Thomson, *The Jack Pine*

EIGHT MILES FROM ESTEN LAKE

5:15 a.m.
eight miles down the trail
lakes stand still
silence and mist
unbearably close to breathing

two loons
methodically work
the south shore of the pond,
dive and break surface
forty feet away and appear nervous,
but continue feeding

6:45 a.m.
return to town
soaking in the sounds of birds,
the dank smell of morning,
trying to bring it all back
to where it just doesn't belong

WAYNE KEON

THE FOGHORN

The foghorn

and the fog
roll in together

No mountains show
out there
this morning
and one by one
the islands disappear

Now even
the great dead maple
where the kingfisher waits
moves
into mist
joins
the white silence stretched
between
long aching calls
and emptiness

RONA MURRAY

F. H. Varley, *Mountains*

THE ISLANDS

There are two of them:

One larger, with steep granite
cliffs facing us, dropping sheer
to the deep lake;

the other smaller, closer
to land, with a reef running
out from it and dead trees
grey, waist-high in the water.

MARGARET ATWOOD

20

Lawren S. Harris, *Pic Island*

F. H. Varley, *Dead Tree, Garibaldi Park*

THE HOLD UP

Stripped of leaves,
surprised —
the trees
scrape the grey winter sky
with veined brittle arms.

M. NOURBESE PHILIP

POEM FOR THE ANCIENT TREES

I
am young and
I want to live
to be old
and I don't want to
outlive these trees — this forest.
When my last song is gone
I want these same trees
to be singing on — newer green songs
for generations to come
so let me be old — let me grow
to be ancient
to come as an elder
before these same temple-green sentinels
with my aged limbs
and still know a wonder
that will outlast me.
O I want
long love
long life.
Give me
150 years
of luck.
But don't
let me
outlive
these trees.

ROBERT PRIEST

A.Y. Jackson, *First Snow Algoma*

FALL

A stiff breeze shakes the summer
Red-blistered leaves rake into piles
A spark sheds black ash everywhere

The first snow guards the hillside
Like the white wrist of winter
The fist is not far behind

DOUG BEARDSLEY

Tom Thomson, *First Snow in Autumn*

Lawren S. Harris, *First Snow, North Shore of Lake Superior*

FREEZE-UP

I wonder at what exact moment
(I wish I'd been there)
something or someone said
"That's the very last drop going over."

And the startled waterfall
suddenly couldn't budge
and knew it was so.

RAYMOND SOUSTER

HAIKU

My roof was once firm
yet now it cannot even
keep the stars out.

CHRISTOPHER DEWDNEY

FEAR OF THE LANDSCAPE

On a hot morning
walking through rough thicket,
bushes and rocks
close to the bluffs
I was uneasy and clung to things.
The sound of a cricket
or the calls of birds were shrill
lesions in the quiet air
around me, sweltering and still.
The leaves hung from the trees
dangling on thin stems.

I am walking quickly and the land
stops. The ground
drops to a beach of stones
where a silent boat leans at the shore
into a sandy mound,
its stiff poled oars
outstretched.
The lake gulls circling it
cry out in the heat.
The sound of dry breath clings to me.
I hear the sun's core burn.
Have I been too long in cities
that I have such fear
of the landscape?

IAN YOUNG

Franz Johnston, *Fire-swept, Algoma*

Tom Thomson, *Bateaux*

SONG

The sun is mine
And the trees are mine
The light breeze is mine
And the birds that inhabit the air
are mine
Their voices upon the wind
are in my ear

ROBERT HOGG

SURPRISE

I feel like the ground in winter,
Hard, cold, dark, dead, unyielding.

Then hope pokes through me
Like a crocus.

JEAN LITTLE

MAPLES

How much of magic
still lies between

first-sipped rain
and the soon-to-follow

branch-shy showing
of the buds?

RAYMOND SOUSTER

F. H. Varley, *Three Clouds and a Tree*

F. H. Varley, *Tree Tufts*

THE GROUP OF SEVEN

When Group of Seven member A.Y. Jackson was a young artist, an elderly woman once said to him, "It's bad enough to have to live in this country, without having pictures of it in your home."

What kind of pictures did many Canadians want early in the twentieth century? Gentle scenes of country life — cattle in the fields, great banks of harmless clouds, pretty sunrises and prettier sunsets — that looked very little like Canada.

The Group of Seven wanted to change all that. They wanted to paint the harshness of Canada, the unpretty beauty of it. For them, experiencing the land firsthand was the only way to understand it and to paint it. Members of the Group and their friends took camping and sketching trips to the wilderness. Their guide and inspiration was Tom Thomson, a painter who lived part of each year in Algonquin Park, painting with great rough brushfuls of colour that captured the wild, beautiful land around him. (In 1917 Thomson drowned in Canoe Lake, which he had painted several times. Many people believe he was murdered.)

In 1920, the Group had their first exhibition. One critic dismissed them as "crazy"; but many others liked their work, and soon the Group had changed the way Canadians saw our land — and ourselves. The Group believed that "art must grow and flower in the land before the country will be a real home for its people."

Today, when we describe what "home" means to us, the paintings of Tom Thomson and the Group of Seven are among the first images that come to mind.

The original members of the Group of Seven were Franklin Carmichael, Lawren S. Harris, A.Y. Jackson, Franz Johnston, Arthur Lismer, J.E.H. MacDonald and F.H. Varley. Later they invited three others to join them: A.J. Casson, L.L. Fitzgerald and Edwin Holgate.

After their final exhibition, in 1931, each artist went his own way, knowing that together they had created a uniquely Canadian artistic identity.

Lawren S. Harris, *Mt. Lefroy*

CREDITS

PAINTINGS

Carmichael, Franklin (1890–1945)
page 5   *The Glade* 1922
oil on canvas
63.9 x 76.7 cm
University College Art Collection, University of Toronto
(Photo: John Glover, University of Toronto)

page 18   *Mirror Lake* 1929
watercolour on paper
44.0 x 54.5 cm
McMichael Canadian Art Collection
Gift of Mr. and Mrs. R.G. Mastin
1976.8

Casson, A.J. (1898–1992)
page 3   *White Pine* c. 1957
oil on canvas
76.0 x 101.3 cm
McMichael Canadian Art Collection
Gift of the Founders, Robert and Signe McMichael
1966.16.119

Harris, Lawren S. (1885–1970)
page 7   *Montreal River* c. 1920
oil on pressed board
27.0 x 34.7 cm
McMichael Canadian Art Collection
Gift of the Founders, Robert and Signe McMichael
1966.16.77

page 8   *Above Lake Superior* c. 1922
oil on canvas
121.9 x 152.4 cm
Art Gallery of Ontario, Toronto
Gift from the Reuben and Kate Leonard Canadian Fund, 1929
Acc. No. 13350
(Photo: Larry Ostrom, Art Gallery of Ontario)

page 9   *Snow II* 1915
oil on canvas
120.3 x 127.3 cm
National Gallery of Canada, Ottawa
Acc. No. 1193

page 21   *Pic Island* 1923
oil on panel
30.1 x 37.9 cm
McMichael Canadian Art Collection
Gift of the Founders, Robert and Signe McMichael
1973.14.1

page 25   *First Snow, North Shore of Lake Superior* 1923
oil on canvas
123.0 x 153.3 cm
Vancouver Art Gallery, Founders Fund
Acc. No. VAG 50.4
(Photo: Trevor Mills)

page 30   *Mt. Lefroy* 1930
oil on canvas
133.5 x 153.5 cm
McMichael Canadian Art Collection
Purchase 1975
1975.7

Jackson, A.Y. (1882–1974)
page 2   *The Edge of the Maple Wood* 1910

oil on canvas
54.6 x 65.4 cm
National Gallery of Canada, Ottawa
Acc. No. 4298
Reproduced courtesy Dr. Naomi Jackson Groves

page 14   *Algoma, November* c. 1935
oil on canvas
81.3 x 102.1 cm
National Gallery of Canada, Ottawa
Gift of H.S. Southam, Ottawa, 1945
Acc. No. 4611
Reproduced courtesy Dr. Naomi Jackson Groves

page 15   *Maple Woods, Algoma* 1920
oil on canvas
63.5 x 81.5 cm
Art Gallery of Ontario, Toronto
Purchased 1981 with funds raised in 1977 by the volunteer
    committee (matched by Wintario) to celebrate the
    opening of the Canadian Wing
Acc. No. 81115
Reproduced courtesy Dr. Naomi Jackson Groves

page 24   *First Snow Algoma* c. 1919–20
oil on canvas
107.1 x 127.7 cm
McMichael Canadian Art Collection
In memory of Gertrude Wells Hilborn
1966.7
Reproduced courtesy Dr. Naomi Jackson Groves

Johnston, Franz (1888–1949)
page 26   *Fire-swept, Algoma* 1920
oil on canvas
127.5 x 167.5 cm
National Gallery of Canada, Ottawa
Acc. No. 1694

Lismer, Arthur (1885–1969)
jacket   *The Guide's Home, Algonquin* 1914
oil on canvas
102.6 x 114.4 cm
National Gallery of Canada, Ottawa
Acc. No. 1155

MacDonald, J.E.H. (1873–1932)
page 1   *Leaves in the Brook* 1919
oil on canvas
52.7 x 65.0 cm
McMichael Canadian Art Collection
Gift of the Founders, Robert and Signe McMichael
1966.16.32

page 11   *The Tangled Garden* 1916
oil on beaverboard
121.4 x 152.4 cm
National Gallery of Canada, Ottawa
Gift of W.M. Southam, F.N. Southam and H.S. Southam, 1937,
    in memory of their brother Richard Southam

Thomson, Tom (1877–1917)
page 6   *Northern River* c. 1914–c. 1915
oil on canvas
115.1 x 102.0 cm
National Gallery of Canada, Ottawa
Acc. No. 1055

page 10   *Wildflowers* 1917
oil on panel
21.6 x 26.8 cm
McMichael Canadian Art Collection

Gift of Mr. R.A. Laidlaw
1970.12.2

page 17   *Summer Day* 1916
oil on panel
21.6 x 26.8 cm
McMichael Canadian Art Collection
Gift of R.A. Laidlaw
1966.15.18

page 19   *The Jack Pine* 1916–1917
oil on canvas
127.9 x 139.8 cm
National Gallery of Canada, Ottawa
Acc. No. 1519

page 25   *First Snow in Autumn* c. 1912–c. 1913
oil on wood
12.8 x 18.2 cm
National Gallery of Canada, Ottawa
Bequest of Dr. J.M. MacCallum, Toronto, 1944
Acc. No. 4670

page 27   *Bateaux* c. 1916
oil on panel
21.6 x 26.7 cm
Art Gallery of Ontario, Toronto
Gift from the Reuben and Kate Leonard Canadian Fund, 1927
Acc. No. 853

Varley, F.H. (1881–1969)
page 12   *Above Arctic Bay* 1938
pencil and watercolour on paper
21.6 x 29.8 cm
The Montreal Museum of Fine Arts Collection
1942.766
(Photo: Brian Merrett, MBAM)
Reproduced courtesy Mrs. D. McKay / F.H. Varley Estate

page 13   *Eskimo Tents — Cape Dorset* 1938
charcoal and watercolour on paper
22.8 x 30.5 cm
National Archives of Canada, Ottawa
Reproduced courtesy Mrs. D. McKay / F.H. Varley Estate

page 20   *Mountains* c. 1957
graphite on buff wove paper
20.0 x 27.7 cm
National Gallery of Canada, Ottawa
Gift from the Douglas M. Duncan Collection, 1970
Acc. No. 16143
Reproduced courtesy Mrs. D. McKay / F.H. Varley Estate

page 22   *Dead Tree, Garibaldi Park* c. 1928
oil on panel on plywood
30.3 x 38.1 cm
McMichael Canadian Art Collection
Gift of the Founders, Robert and Signe McMichael
1966.16.142
Reproduced courtesy Mrs. D. McKay / F.H. Varley Estate

page 28   *Three Clouds and a Tree* c. 1935
oil on wood
30.1 x 38.0 cm
National Gallery of Canada, Ottawa
Gift from the Douglas M. Duncan Collection, 1970
Acc. No. 16503 (Douglas Duncan #4147; Varley Inventory #203)
Reproduced courtesy Mrs. D. McKay / F.H. Varley Estate

page 29   *Tree Tufts* c. 1935
oil on wood
30.5 x 37.8 cm
National Gallery of Canada, Ottawa
Acc. No. 6513 (Varley Inventory #1180)
Reproduced courtesy Mrs. D. McKay / F.H. Varley Estate

INDEX